The Average Joe's Guide to Success

The Brilliant Overachievers Will Never See You Coming

R. C. Farrington

Illustrated by Jason Farrington

ISBN-13: 978-0692945247
ISBN-10: 0692945245
Library of Congress Control Number: 2017916045
CreateSpace Independent Publishing Platform, North
Charleston, SC

To all those average Joes and Josies who have watched overachievers dominate the world of business. Don't be discouraged—there is a burning light at the end of the tunnel.

A special thank-you to Greg Farrington for his contributions to this guide.

A special thank-you to Greg Farrington for his contributions to this guide.

Contents

Introduction

Throughout our lives, we're under pressure to excel, and maybe, if we fall into the select group of one in a hundred thousand overachievers, we just might have a chance for success. Unfortunately, at a fairly early age, most of us realize we're not straight-A students and we are not going to graduate at the top of our class. We're not great at sports and were never meant to be pro athletes. We weren't born with a silver spoon in our mouths, and there is no family business to join.

Throughout this guide, I will reference overachievers countless times. I am not looking at them in a negative light. After all, in the subtitle, I refer to them as "brilliant." But where does that leave the rest of us?

Yes, you may be average, but so what? So are millions of other people. It's not a question of accepting that you're average; it's a matter of knowing your own capabilities and strengths and doing something about them.

You are undervalued, underrated, and underappreciated, but it's your responsibility to change that—to decide where you want to go and how to get there. Oh yes, and you need the willingness to work hard to achieve your goals.

Are you going to be a multimillionaire? Probably not, but there's nothing wrong being a thousandaire. Yes, I did just say that. The Urban Dictionary definition is as follows: "One whose wealth is estimated at a thousand (as of dollars or pounds). Being a thousandaire is having the attitude of a millionaire, with a touch of bling." Alternatively, what about having the home of your dreams or traveling around the world? For the average Joe or Josie, there are no get-rich-quick schemes. The bottom line is this: your only limitation is you.

But there is hope, especially for all of us average Joes. Get out of your comfort zone, level the playing field, and compete for those better-paying jobs and promotions.

Some people compete in the world of business with very little effort and have great success, while others find themselves left behind when the same opportunity arises.

Many would say, "So what? It's a dog-eat-dog world out there. The spoils go to the victor. That's the way the world turns." I beg to differ.

There are many of us who may never be the CEO of a company or even find a position in upper management, much less make millions of dollars. Just because things don't come easily for us, that doesn't mean we can't pull ourselves up by our bootstraps and move up much higher in a company's organization. For average Joes or Josies like us, we have to work harder and smarter. We also have to reflect on our inner selves and learn to cultivate and maximize those good attributes we already possess—and maybe develop a few new ones that will help us become more successful in the business world.

While writing this book, I've had several friends and family members all echo the same opinion. They say the concept of this book is great, but they don't see me as an average Joe. I'm flattered, but they are so wrong in their opinions it's not even funny.

The truth is, what they see in me is the result of an average Joe using his determination, imagination, and grit to get the job done. They are missing the point that in fact I was, still am, and will always be an average Joe. I am surrounded by people who are smarter than me, but I am not intimidated by that. I will always move forward and achieve my goals where I can, as should you.

This book is not a scientific study of being average. Instead, it is the summation over a wide span of time on how an average person can achieve his or her goals. Nothing in this guide will promise you huge financial rewards. It is, however, a guide to help you use your mind and your God-given talents to achieve your goals throughout life, even if you're not a genius or an overachiever. I've always said that life is an adventure and that you can do better than you think.

Yes, this is an adventure of an average Joe who, with all his shortcomings, has not only survived but excelled by allowing his imagination and other attributes to become part of his everyday life.

This is a guide and not an encyclopedia for success. It is a quick read and gets right to the point. You will not be overwhelmed with mountains of information you have to remember. As you read this guide, you'll find that many components and attributes are needed to accomplish your success goals. Some of the components are not attributes, but they are just as important. You may find that not everything discussed is relevant to you and your career path, but most things will be. I have also tried to include other thoughts and realities that will be useful at some point in your path to success. Some of these thoughts may be considered fringe areas, but I believe they will be just as helpful for you to achieve your goals.

This guide was written with a goal of revving up your inner engines for self-improvement. Everything I will be discussing in this guide is predicated on you motivating yourself to a new level. At the end of most of the chapters, you'll find a notes page where you can write down any inspired thoughts that may help propel you in your quest for success. As an average Joe or Josie, you will have to work harder and smarter, but I know that if the drive is there, you'll be successful.

It's OK to Be Average

Let's start out with the basics. Yes, it really is OK to be average. Where we get into trouble is when we accept the notion that being average means someone is willing to accept less or be less.

In case you haven't already figured out, I'm also very average. There's no reason to dwell on that fact negatively, because it's not negative.

There is nothing wrong with accepting the fact that you're average (after all, most of us are). But never let that become an excuse not to improve yourself and your position in life.

Being average can mean you are someone who plays it safe. No one can call you a failure, but at the same time, no one can call you a success. In a way, it's a safe and secure state of being. I contend, however, that given the chance, most average Joes or Josies would like to improve and increase their earning power.

For me, my glass is never half empty; it's always half full. Based on my observations, I sense that many average Joes and Josies view their glasses as half empty. On the surface, a half-empty glass doesn't sound too bad. Maybe there's less chance of spilling it and making a mess of things. But this one little statement has a great impact on your life. Like it or not, you might view things more negatively than positively. You might be looking backward or not past today instead of looking forward. You might not see the light at the end of the tunnel—instead, you see only a cold, dark tunnel. My comments may sound harsh, but if you really look deep into yourself and your glass is half empty, then this is a wake-up call for a successful future in the business world.

To compete with overachievers, average Joes and Josies need every positive edge. To succeed, we must see our glasses as half full, with the opportunity to fill them up even further. In today's business climate, companies are looking for positive-thinking people who have the mind-set to help them achieve their goals.

As we go deeper into this guide, please remember this is not an autobiography, but an opportunity for me to make my points based on my past experiences. I have related my own life's journey to prove what I say is believable.

The Early Years

Now that I've reflected, the earliest sign of my averageness dates back to the fourth grade. That was the year my school assigned students to different levels for reading and spelling classes. To my dismay, I was placed down to the third-grade level for spelling class.

Although I do remember the actual name of my spelling teacher, you will get the gist of her behavior through the fictitious name I'm going to give her. Ms. Crabapple was a well-seasoned teacher who had an ironclad approach to spelling. I remember getting my knuckles rapped by her wooden ruler. I truly can't imagine what a mild, quiet student like me could have done to incur her wrath. Well, on second thought, maybe I do, but that's for another time. The things I hated the most were her big, bold, red checkmarks on my papers each week after I took her spelling tests.

Ms. Crabapple's technique to improve spelling failed to work on me. I couldn't understand it, or maybe I just didn't pay attention. I think at the end of the year she passed me just so she wouldn't have to have me in class the next year.

I coasted through junior high (now called middle school), and I was happy just getting by, without thoughts of anything else. Of course, my grades reflected that: just average. Poor spelling habits followed me all the way through high school and college.

In my early years of business, to make up for my poor spelling, I purchased a twenty-five-thousand-word dictionary. After all these years, I still have it. However, I haven't used it since spell check was developed for word-processing programs, but it's a good reminder for me.

The point of all this is that even though my spelling skills were below average, I learned to use tools to help me in the business world. Really, I should have taken a class to learn how to spell better as an adult, but I suppose my ego got in the way. Nonetheless, I found tools to help me compete.

By the time I reached high school, two events got my attention. One was more impactful than the other. The first event was an aptitude test. Here again, although they meant well, the schools were trying to pigeonhole students—or, in their minds, help guide them toward their futures. I tested at the ninety-eighth percentile in mechanical aptitude and was enrolled in the vocational technical curriculum. Back then, that meant training as a car mechanic or air-conditioning-service technician. There is nothing wrong with that, but for me, I could not see a job like that in my future.

When the guidance counselor gave me the results of the aptitude test and asked me to sign the acceptance form, I refused. I went on to tell him that I had decided I wanted to go on to college after graduating high school. He refused my request, stating that my grades and aptitude-test results would not allow that. By the way, did I mention that my counselor, who was deciding my future, was really a PE coach? Finally, I agreed to enroll in the general-studies curriculum. I knew this would still allow me a chance of getting into college.

The second event, whose significance would not sink in for years, was the personality test I took in high school. Most people are either introverts or extroverts—oh, but not me. Yes, I tested dead center, right in the middle. I was an ambivert (and this word doesn't even exist in most personality discussions).

My natural state of being tended to the introverted side, but I discovered when I needed to speak in front of people or express my opinion, I would lean on my extroverted side. It's a worthwhile process to find out where you are on the personality chart, although most of you who swing to the far left or the far right probably already know your type.

My college years were also a confirmation of my averageness. I graduated with a bachelor of science degree in general management with a 2.5 GPA. Now that you know I'm average, let's get on with the guide.

Notes

Be Inquisitive

Francis Bacon said, "Knowledge is power." That statement is as true today as it was four hundred years ago when he made the statement.

Ask questions, but ask the right kind of questions. As an up-and-comer, it's good to ask questions. Some say I ask too many questions, but in some industries, the information you need to know may not be readily available. Asking questions about the business or industry you're in will also show your superiors you're interested. In fact, if you're lucky, you may find a superior who will enjoy imparting information to you.

Some may say that asking questions is a sign of weakness or a lack of understanding of the business you work in. To a degree, they might be right if you're not asking the right kind of questions. Remember to think before you ask. The more thought-provoking the question, the better the response will be. This is a good time to remind you to be a good listener. Maybe some of your questions will be answered before you even ask them.

Years ago, I found myself blessed to work for a visionary in his industry. He was the most down-to-earth man you would ever know, and he was very frank. He enjoyed spending time with his employees. The man was John Cotter, the founder of Cotter & Company. You may know him better as the founder of True Value hardware stores. Back in those days, the sales volume of the company was in excess of $1 billion. Over a five-year period, I was able to sit down with him in private on several occasions. In each meeting, I somehow overcame the overwhelming inclination to just sit there and stare; I was able ask him a few questions in each meeting. Thank goodness he was quick to pick up on the silence and help carry the conversation.

One conversation we had was about his vision of having True Value stores pay Cotter & Company, their hardware supplier, electronically. This was years before electronic payments became a reality. It seemed such a futuristic thought to me at the time, but it's now commonplace. The old saying that a man like that has forgotten more than you will ever know is so true. I will always cherish my conversations with Mr. Cotter. So remember: never pass up an opportunity to learn from your superiors. This is the type of knowledge you will never get out of a textbook.

Having just said that, I believe the next best thing to asking questions is using Google to find the answer. The Internet has a tremendous wealth of information on any subject. There is no excuse not to tap into that resource. I can't tell you how many books I have purchased over the years for research on certain subjects, but my bookshelf looks impressive. I could have saved big dollars surfing the Internet. There is rarely a day when I'm not personally researching a topic or a question that relates to the business world.

Always be like a sponge, and absorb knowledge—whatever the source. Even if you can't use it today, someday it may be valuable.

Notes

Imagine That

If we look at personal attributes, imagination is my strongest. This is one area where I will admit that I just might be above average. Each of us is different, and even average Joes have areas they can admit to being very good at. Mine just happens to be my imagination. So whatever yours is, take advantage of it, and use it to your full advantage.

In my reality, my imagination is as real as I am. It doesn't make any difference what I'm doing—working, playing, talking, or sleeping—my imagination is always with me and is as much a part of my life as breathing. It's not something that's stored away somewhere in my hidden self, waiting to be beckoned. Just as I see, hear, move, and think, my imagination is there and part of my every breathing moment. This allows me to envision things I see in the business world not for what they are but for what they could be.

I've learned over the years there are different types of imagination. The most common viewpoint of imagination is the *Merriam-Webster's Collegiate Dictionary* definition, which states it is "the act or power of forming a mental image of something not present to the senses or never before wholly perceived in reality." In other words, from a business perspective, you create in your mind a vision, product, or direction that will help you and your company grow.

The BASF Corporation slogan is a good way to look at another form of imagination: "We don't make a lot of the products you buy. We make a lot of the products you buy better."

My version, I would say, goes something like this: "I may not have been the person who put forth a good idea for the company, but I will always try my best to make these ideas better."

People with strong imaginations need to understand that other people also come up with good ideas, concepts, and proposals. You don't want to be like the overachievers and always try to one-up others. This will leave you in an adversarial role with your coworkers. Instead, use your imagination to improve on their ideas; make them better. This way, you don't alienate anyone, and it demonstrates to your superiors you're a team player and a positive thinker.

The imagination is such a powerful tool in your personal-attribute arsenal for the business world, and I can't say enough about it. To be honest, I might not be able to explain how to develop your imagination, because mine developed at a very early age and is available whenever I need it. In fact, it pops up without warning.

Growing up, I was lucky that my father managed a lumberyard. He was always bringing home scrap lumber and nails, which gave me a chance to build things from my imagination. I was even luckier that my mother would allow these monstrosities I built in the backyard to stay there. One month I would build an Old West army fort. The next month, I would build a two-story flying fortress. This process also allowed me to imagine adventures to go along with what I had built.

When I was a very young adult, the digital revolution was just beginning. The Atari, Commodore 64, and Texas Instrument TI-99 game and computer systems had just arrived. I loved the games, but I really got hooked playing with the TI-99. The thought of creating programs was fascinating to me. The only computer class I had in college taught me how to write programs on keypunch cards. Don't worry if you don't know what a keypunch card is—neither does anyone else. It's not worth another sentence to explain.

Here again, my imagination went wild. I quickly learned that there was nothing I couldn't do with a computer by writing my own programs. Although math is a huge part of programming, I realized early on that this average Joe could still accomplish what I needed to without using scientific algorithms and sticking to the basic math that I understood. My algebra and geometry instructors from high school would have been disappointed.

I know what you're thinking: "So what? You learned to program as a hobby." Well, that is true; it started out a hobby, but over the years, it turned into a point-of-sale software business. I eventually sold the rights to the software for a modest amount. By the way, this point-of-sale software is still used twenty-five years later. The point is, an average Joe (or Josie) can turn his (or her) hobby into something that will help improve the future.

Using my imagination has enhanced my abilities in the world of business and helped me earn additional income that otherwise I might have never earned.

Sometimes a single attribute like imagination can open other doors for you. As another hobby, I got the itch to write adventure novels. Because writing does not come naturally to me, I will never win any type of literary awards. In fact, most book critics and reviewers will never give me much more than an average rating for my novels. Luckily my readers are much more generous with their reviews and ratings. Fitting for an average Joe, right? I view myself more as a storyteller of adventures. As an independent author, my eleven novels have sold about eight to ten thousand copies. It's nothing to write home about, but then again, it requires using my imagination and is a way to create additional income.

Because I'm deeply involved in advertising and marketing, my imagination has been the perfect attribute to assist me in these endeavors. Actually, if it weren't for my imagination, I would not be involved in advertising and marketing. Imagination and creativity go hand in hand in these fields. To me, creativity is taking an idea that came from the imagination and bringing it to life. My artistic talents have never passed the first-grade level, so I'll never be able to create a finished product in the advertising world with my artistic abilities. However, I can still use my talents to describe what I want to design and let a graphic designer assist me.

I use my imagination every day in my profession. None of what I've mentioned have been multimillion-dollar producers, but they have helped me compete in a million-dollar business climate in a way I otherwise could not have.

Notes

Challenge Yourself

In the previous chapter, I glossed over my journey into software development. It had a profound effect on my career path. The software has indirectly and directly followed me through four companies. In some cases, I evolved around the software, and in other cases, it was the point-of-sale concept that drove me in my career. This may sound confusing, but I'll clear this up quickly.

When computer programming was still a hobby for me, I was working in sales for a hardware distributor. Although I was extremely excited about programming, I was desperate to find a business use for it. One day it hit me like a ton of bricks, and I knew what I wanted to develop. Back then, the small mom-and-pop hardware stores and lumberyards were facing a new competitor. Yes, it was the big-box stores. Although what were thought of as megastores back then have long been replaced by even bigger box stores, they were still killing off the small stores. These small stores desperately needed help to survive. They needed automation! Most of them still did everything with a pad and pencil.

There were automation systems for these stores at the time, but there was a problem. The systems were expensive. Their base price was at least $80,000. If the big boxes didn't put small stores out of business, the cost of automation would. These stores desperately needed an affordable software solution in order to survive. So this average Joe now had a focus: design an affordable software system that would help these small retailers survive. Having the knowledge of the hardware and lumber business was also a huge asset to me in developing software.

I spent about a year writing the point-of-sale software to automate a hardware store. This was done in my spare time and cost me only my time. Once the software was ready, I needed to find a hardware store to help me test the software. A few months later, I found the perfect candidate. It was a very small rural hardware store that had just purchased a Tandy Radio Shack computer and wasn't quite sure what to do with it. Between us, we bought the hardware needed to turn his computer into a point-of-sale system. In a couple of months, his system was checking out customers and handling his inventory and receivables. This is a case where two average Joes had done the unthinkable. A year later, I was able to automate hardware stores and lumberyards with a bare-bones system that would cost the stores about $5,000, including software and hardware.

I saw a need that the market was not addressing, and, at very little cost, I went for it. Over the years, I have automated tiny mom-and-pop stores into very large megastores. It was never easy for me, but I hung in there and never gave up. This adventure in software opened many new doors and gave me opportunities to expand my horizons into other areas. To date, software is still a part of my life—but only a part. For me, it's a building block that allows me to succeed at future challenges.

These are some of the building blocks of a successful challenge:

1. Find a real need in an area that is begging for improvement. It's wise to pick an area where you have experience and understanding. This can be something personal or incorporated within your career path.

2. Develop a realistic plan of action to address the need. Remember, if you can't implement the plan, then nothing will be accomplished.

3. Be ready to endure setbacks and lack of interest from others. Sometimes others may not see your vision. As they say, "Patience is a virtue." It won't be easy, and it won't happen overnight.

4. Be open-minded to change. For you to be successful, your plans may have to change. What you start out with and what you end up with may be very different.

5. Protect your work. If you're doing something within your career path, make sure others can't claim it as theirs. If it's outside of work, you may need a

patent, copyright, or trademark. And you should at least get an attorney's advice.

Notes

Always Move Forward

A positive person tends to look forward toward the future, whereas a negative person tends to look backward at the past or just lives in the day-to-day. To be successful, you need to understand that nothing stands still. You must always look forward toward the future. If you stand still, you are really going backward, and the overachievers will pass you by.

In this fast-paced world of ever-changing technology, it's sometimes difficult to keep abreast of everything. At least try to keep up with your particular industry and any development that relates to it.

There is another side of this coin to think about. Sometimes it's OK to stop and smell the roses. If you accomplish something, you should take time and reflect on your success. Take notes, and be prepared to fine-tune what you have accomplished.

The overachievers, on the other hand, tend to never stop. As soon as they succeed at their plan or goal, they're off to the next challenge. Sometimes a successful plan needs time to fully develop to meet its full potential. The overachiever will take risks and sometimes chase after the impossible or after a plan that has very little chance of success.

You don't have to chase as many projects as the overachievers do, but the ones you do chase should be done well.

The 2016 movie *The Founder* is a perfect example of three average Joes who created the McDonald's fast-food restaurant chain. As soon as I said McDonald's, you and everyone else in the world instantly thought these men must have been overachievers, not average Joes. True, these three gentlemen revolutionized the fast-food-restaurant business, but it was not because they were overachievers. The reality is that these three men were average Joes who had a very strong desire to succeed and who never gave up.

The point I'm building up to is that the two McDonald brothers achieved success creating the most incredible fast-food restaurant ever dreamed of. Nothing was easy for them; they were driven to painstakingly produce the perfect fast-food restaurant. Once achieving the unthinkable, they were content to stop and smell the roses of success and live happily ever after.

The third average Joe, Ray Kroc, saw their success and was driven by a vision to make this small fast-food restaurant chain an international phenomenon. Nothing ever came easy for Ray Kroc; in fact, he failed many times in his life. His drive to succeed and to always move forward after each success eventually established McDonald's as the largest fast-food-restaurant chain in the world.

Do take time to watch this movie; it is a classic example of what it takes to succeed and reminds us to never stop moving forward.

Notes

Attributes

Merriam-Webster defines the word "attribute" as "a quality, character, or characteristic ascribed to someone or something."

We all have many attributes we can draw from on the journey to success. There are positive ones, and there are negative ones. We have to learn to maximize the positive ones and minimize the negative ones—not to mention develop new ones. As mentioned before, one of my strongest attributes happens to be imagination. Just think: if you, an average Joe or Josie, magnify four to ten positive attributes and minimize those negative attributes you're carrying around as excess baggage, those overachievers would be dust in your rearview mirror.

Attributes, when you think about them, are almost endless. I'll cover a small list of positive ones and negative ones to get your thought process going. You should be able to add many more to the list of positive ones.

Positive attributes:

1. Being an achiever: Setting goals and accomplishing them is important. Achieving your daily assignments and projects is just as important. Being an achiever means being able to do what you say you're going to do. You'll be known as the go-to person for your company to get the job done.

2. Consistency: When you're consistent at a high level of work, supervisors will notice. This also helps you set your own bar of expectations. A consistent performer is one your company can count on.

49

3. Flexibility: This means being able to change and see other people's viewpoints and take different approaches to problems or opportunities. Many times, in the business world, things don't go your way. You have to accept that and move on.

4. Listening skills: A good listener is always much better than a good talker. By taking the time to hear someone else, you will be much better off formulating your own plans or thoughts. You will find out that many times, the other person will have helpful thoughts and comments.

5. Imagination: This is thoroughly covered in a previous chapter.

6. Inventiveness: This is very close to imagination. Being able to create ideas and plans—not just things—is very important in the world of business.

7. Open-mindedness: Seeing both sides of discussions and not having your mind made up in advance can be great attributes to have. When things get emotional, sometimes we shut down these attributes. We need to learn to keep an open mind even when times get tough.

8. Organization: Organization is key in getting ahead. Most people fail at this. Planning and being prepared will give you a huge edge in business. Do not underrate this attribute.

9. Patience: Having patience in yourself and others is very important. Not everyone thinks or moves at

your pace. Take time to let a plan unfold, and don't try to rush it along. Never use patience as an excuse for not doing something.

10. Positivity: Being a positive person in the business world is such a plus. Supervisors love this attribute. This is also very good for your well-being. A positive attitude is contagious.

11. Practicality: Being practical and realistic is great as long as you don't let this attribute overshadow your inventiveness and imagination. This might take a balancing act, but is very worthwhile. A practical approach will keep you grounded and on target.

12. Responsibility: Responsibility for your actions and taking ownership for your job and assignments are key. This attribute is so simple to understand and

do; however, it's shocking to see how many people never get this one.

13. Adaptability: Sometimes you need to be able to adapt and make changes to get the job done. There is nothing wrong with being adaptable. Actually, it's a great attribute. Your superiors will see that you are capable of thinking outside the box.

I have also listed twelve negative attributes. Except for one, there is no need to discuss them. These are negative attributes you don't want.

Negative attributes

1. Aggression: Many, including overachievers, would consider this attribute a positive one. Maybe it is; but for me, it's not. Being aggressive might not always work. When the wrong people try to use this

attribute, they can set off emotions that may not contribute to their well-being. I would not want this one in my arsenal of positive attributes.

2. Arrogance

3. Bossiness

4. Impatience

5. Impulsivity

6. Inconsideration

7. Indecisiveness

8. Being overcritical

9. Pessimism

10. Quick-temperedness

11. Tactlessness

12. Vengefulness

Attributes make up a large portion of the key ingredients in your mission to be successful. These building blocks reflect your strengths and where you should focus as you begin to move your career forward. Whether your goal is to grow with your current company or to seek a new company to expand your career, these are the building blocks of your future.

Notes

The Competitive Drive

Having a competitive nature has never hurt anyone in the business world. Even being slightly competitive will help you in your quest to improve yourself. For some, being competitive may originate in participating in sports or even being a spectator. For others, it has nothing to do with sports. Some people just have the drive to go after whatever lies in front of them. I would say that most overachievers have a very high competitive drive, whereas most average Joes are probably more laid-back.

Think about it this way: If you're sitting at home watching your favorite sports team, and they score a goal, you typically react in a very positive way. You might yell, cheer, or even jump up and down. That's the feeling of competitive spirit. Take that to work with you, and your enthusiasm will begin to show. As you accomplish projects, you will want to accomplish more and more, and your superiors will take notice.

Years ago, during my college years, I had a part-time job at a very large department store for the Christmas season. Halfway through the season, the department manager told me, "I like the way you work. The more you do for the store, the more I'm going to ask you to do." I had a hard time understanding his comment. It seemed counterproductive to me back then, but when the first of January rolled around, I received my answer loud and clear. Out of 200 part-time Christmas employees, 198 were laid off. I was one of two employees who were retained. The bottom line was that my drive to do more than the position required did not get me a promotion, but it kept me employed when others were not. And I was very motivated at the time. To attend college, I had to pay my own tuition.

In order to move up in the corporate world, you cannot just put in your time each week and go home. If you do, the overachievers will eat you alive. Depending on the circumstances, sometimes you will just have to work harder.

If you want to be noticed in a positive light, having drive and enthusiasm is a great way to get noticed. Of course, you must first ensure you are producing positive results at work.

Notes

_____

_____

_____

_____

_____

_____

_____

_____

_____

_____

_____

_____

The Struggle

No one ever said life would be easy. That is so true. We look at others and ask, "How did they do that?" Or we wonder, "Boy, were they at the right place at the right time!" I suppose that can happen, but most of the time, unless you're in the lucky-sperm club, it's a struggle to be successful. The overachievers might make it look easy from an outsider's perspective, but it's actually not.

Over the years, I can't tell you how many times I've failed or underperformed based on my own expectations. But each day is a new day for me. Even if one day I found myself beaten down to a 1 on a scale of 1 to 10, the next morning I wake up to a number 10 and start another day. When you're beaten down, don't let yourself stay down for the count. Shake it off, and look at each day as a fresh start.

The loftiest goal I ever set for myself spanned a fifteen-year time frame. I determined to reach this personal goal by the time I was thirty-five years old. During those fifteen years, I never gave up on my dream. Well, guess what? When I woke up on my thirty-fifth birthday, had I made it? No. I didn't even come close to attaining my goal. The truth is, I had the will and a few of the tools, but that was about it. Maybe it was more of a wish goal for my ego.

As I look back at this average Joe, at that moment in time, I realize I had not yet developed the attributes I needed. Over time, my skill sets grew, and eventually, I was able to attain that goal; I turned the wish into a reality. Not attaining your goals does not mean you are a failure; it simply means you didn't achieve those goals. Between the ages of twenty and thirty-five, I still achieved other goals and became more successful each year. I may not have made it to Mount Everest that year, but I made my way up past the foothills.

Even if you fail on occasion, the average Joe can still succeed with drive, determination, and building strong attributes.

The old saying "The harder I work, the luckier I get" really does not make much sense on the surface. However, what it really means is that the harder you work, the more prepared you are and the more you achieve. In that context, I'm a believer.

One of the best times to try new ventures is when you're young and just starting out—but only if you're single, mobile, and fairly debt-free. That's not the case for most young people, though, who are probably married or might have young children. Most likely, both the husband and wife are working…and there's a new home mortgage to contend with…and the story goes on and on. Needless to say, life can be a struggle during this time. Even the overachievers will struggle in such a situation.

It would be easy to give up, just try to survive day by day, and continue being an average Joe in the workplace. At this time in your life, odds are that you're not going to go out and gamble on a new direction or venture. Instead, this is when you dig into your current career and not only make the best of it but also learn everything there is to know about your position and your employer. This will help you succeed in your current job or the next position in the future.

For those just graduating from college, remember that your first career move is probably more of a training ground for you. Take it seriously, and absorb everything you can. Whether you do grow within the company, move on elsewhere in the same industry, or move to a company in a different industry, the experience you acquire will be the building blocks of your future.

I've always said over the years that there are two types of degrees a person can earn. The first one is a college degree, which is a must for us average Joes and Josies, if possible. The next one is just as important: a degree from the business school of hard knocks. We do learn from our own mistakes—after all, trying not to repeat them can be a great motivator—but it's also a lot less painful to learn from others' mistakes and successes. The key is to pay attention and learn to emulate others who are successful, but remember to adapt their behavior to fit your personality. Never try to get ahead in the world trying to be someone else. Be yourself!

Notes

Education

As I stated in the previous chapter, education comes in many forms—from a formal college education to the business school of hard knocks. Unfortunately, many of you may not be in a position to attend college. For whatever reason, college just might not be in the cards. The business school of hard knocks is great for many, but sometimes you're not in the right place at the right time to take advantage of this. There are other ways to advance your knowledge to help you succeed.

Most communities have community colleges that offer a large variety of business courses and two-year associate's degrees in business. Should you attend evening classes, a two-year degree could take several years to earn. Not everyone can make a commitment like this. However, if you do, remember this: whether your degree is a two- or four-year diploma, no one can ever take it away from you. A degree not only helps prepare you for your future in business, but it also sends a clear signal to future employers that you are capable of making long-term commitments. After all, you did commit the time to obtain a degree. When an employer sees that someone has attended night school to earn a degree, it speaks volumes about the character of the person.

There are many of you who may not be able to make such a commitment to attend college on a regular basis. For those who fall in this category, you will need to be more focused in your approach to higher education. You should review the business courses offered by the community college and create a list of classes that relate to your career. This way, you can enroll in one or two classes a semester, keeping the load light while still building a stronger base for your future success. Keep an open mind on courses to take. Some might not even be business-related classes. You might want to consider speech or technology classes to help broaden your horizons and knowledge. What I love about community colleges is that they offer many courses that may not be college accredited but are perfect building blocks for success.

Basic classes to consider include those on the following topics:

1. Business management

2. Marketing and advertising

3. Accounting

4. Business writing

5. Speech and communication

6. Technology

7. Microsoft products

8. Business administration

9. Retail management

10. Systems and network

11. Web design

12. Computer information systems

13. Human-resource management

14. Finance

15. Business statistics

When enrolling in a community college, be sure to spend time with a staff counselor. Let him or her know up front your motivations for attending college and what you hope to get out of the experience. The counselor should be a great asset in guiding you in the right direction.

Notes

The Box

It's easy to say you want to expand your horizons; actually doing it is more difficult. Overachievers are much more open to this concept than us average Joes and Josies. Because of their nature, overachievers will try to do just about anything in the business world to be successful. Sometimes it works, and sometimes it backfires. The average Joe tends not to take risks, so the chance of failure is much lower, as is the chance for success. After all, nothing ventured, nothing gained.

Over the years, there's been much written about "the box"—not "the black box" but "the box." It's the box that we're encouraged to think outside of. The overachievers venture out of the box to think, whereas we average Joes tend to do our thinking inside the box. Over the years, I've discovered that venturing out of the box on occasion can be very rewarding. In fact, I like it so much that I tend to stay out of the box most of the time with my thoughts. Changing your thought process is another tool to add to your success arsenal.

To most people, thinking out of the box is something to talk about, but it may not be a reality. To me, it's using your creative attributes. In the business world, this usually relates to sales, marketing, goals, and management.

Sometimes businesses call it "brainstorming" when it's done in a group of employees. This small think tank or committee meets and throws out different ideas on the table. To many, these processes may sound fake or phony, but the bottom line is that this thought process really works. You just have to let yourself go and not be overly cautious about what you say in the group.

In brainstorming groups, many attributes will come to the surface for you. This is a great place to fine-tune and showcase your talents. Supervisors will notice, especially when many other participants may not buy in to the meeting and stay silent.

Individually thinking outside the box is not something you can always plan on doing, but when it happens, go with the flow. Have a pen and paper ready, and start writing down your thoughts. Go ahead and push the boundaries with your thoughts on the subject at hand.

Remember, many times these thoughts never have a chance to become a reality, but some will. The big benefit from this exercise is that you're training your mind to think creatively, and it's worth the effort. You are truly expanding your horizons.

You will be helping yourself in your quest for success, and you might be surprised when your supervisor starts asking you for your thoughts and opinions.

As businesses grow and expand, they are always looking for middle and upper management. The ideal scenario is to groom future management teams from within the company. However, if the staff of the business is not prepared for this opportunity, the company will not hesitate to look on the outside for the right candidates. This is why if you really want to succeed, you need to be ready when an opportunity presents itself.

You need to develop an opportunistic mind-set to take advantage when promotions are available. The problem is that sometimes you're not aware that the opportunities even exist.

As you expand your horizons, don't be afraid to let upper management know you are sincere about long-term growth opportunities within the company. The door of opportunity does not open very often.

Notes

Goals

All successful companies have many goals and objectives, as should you. If you're in the process of seeking employment, that's a job in itself that requires its own set of goals. The main goal is to find employment. If you're already employed, you should set goals to improve yourself within the company.

You should also set goals for your personal self within the job frame you currently have. I do realize that many companies will issue you a job description, but that is their expectation—not yours. Job descriptions are where many average Joes and Josies get bogged down with blinders. This is also where you might say, "Oh, that's not my job" when a situation arises. I can guarantee you that if you're trying to be successful and move up the corporate ladder, this is not a phrase a supervisor ever wants to hear. You might as well tell him or her, "I'm just here for the paycheck."

Goals for seeking employment:

1. Seek out a strong, growth-oriented company, especially one that is relatively young. There can be good opportunities there. Companies like this are where many of the young overachievers might also be looking for employment. You may have to up your game a little if you find yourself competing with the overachievers. Otherwise, be yourself and demonstrate that you will be a solid contributor in helping the company grow.

2. A solid, well-established company is also good, but it may take longer to advance up the corporate ladder at a company like this. This will be the

typical company you will probably interview with. Most of the positions will be more entry level, with a fairly solid management team already in place. Because of a low turnover in staff, it may take longer to advance. However, if you're motivated you will have an excellent opportunity to learn and build your skills.

Do be careful with an established company that appears to have a high staff turnover rate. This is a big red flag that the company may have serious problems.

3. If this is your first career search, you might seek out a smaller, more regional company to gain some experience and then move on to a stronger company. You probably will make less money and have fewer benefits with this type of company.

However, the tradeoff is a chance to be much closer to the management team, which in turn will accelerate your learning curve.

Goals within your current position:

1. Make sure if you have a job description, you fully understand it and are covering all aspects of the position.

2. Think outside the box and recommend or implement improvements that your supervisors will approve of.

3. Make sure all assignments and projects are always completed accurately and on a timely basis.

4. Be one of the first employees to work each day. Don't ever be known as the last one. Establishing a strong work ethic will help make you a prime candidate for success.

5. Make sure your supervisors are aware of your successes and improvements. There is nothing worse than an unappreciative supervisor. To make it clearer, if your supervisor does not know what you're accomplishing, he or she cannot appreciate what you have done.

6. Ask for more responsibilities and more important assignments. Every company loves an employee who is hungry to produce.

7. Where others point out problems, be the one who offers solutions to those problems. This is a

huge point to remember. Most of your fellow coworkers will not be problem-solvers. You can stand out like a shining star if you embrace this point.

8. Stay positive 100 percent of the time. If you're having a bad day, immerse yourself into your work, and try not to show it. You can always bounce back the next day.

9. Avoid excessive phone calls, Internet surfing, and chatter with fellow employees. If you're motivated to succeed, this will never be a problem.

10. Understand the big picture, and when given the chance, elaborate on it with your supervisors.

11. Always give it your best, and never hold back. If you get caught up in the game of saving ideas to advance yourself for a rainy day, sooner or later that strategy will backfire on you. You will also find yourself sliding back down the corporate ladder as a nonproducer. Go for the gusto every chance you get.

Notes

Take Ownership

This chapter is one of the emotional ones for me. A large
majority of employees of a company never take ownership
of what they do. This is a true buzzkill for employers.
When referring to the company they work for, many
overachievers will use the terms "we" and "us." They're
demonstrating to management that they have bought in to
the company and consider themselves a part of the
company. Other employees who use the terms "they" and
"them" are sending the message that they're just putting in
their forty hours in each week and really don't feel a part of
the company.

I hear people say "This is my project," but when something
goes wrong, they say, "I don't know why they did that."
They're faking ownership. When something goes wrong,
they bail out.

You can't just fake ownership; you have to believe in what you're doing and take a personal interest in the company's well-being. If you can't do that where you are but really believe in this advice, you should move on to another company that you can believe in.

By taking ownership, you're telling the company that you're buying into the company and its goals with your work ethic and determination to help it succeed. When you act as one with your company, believe me, it is noticed and appreciated. This will give you a big leg up with your employer.

When you take genuine ownership of your position, you're really making the statement that it's also your company. Yes, we all know it's actually not, but your chances of advancement and success are much improved if you feel that way. The implicit swagger of ownership will radiate from you.

You need to be proud of your work and its results. Be prepared to stand up for your endeavors. As a supervisor, if I have doubts about an employee who nevertheless feels strongly about his or her proposals, I just might turn that employee loose on the project. A person with that kind of conviction will probably make up for any shortcomings the proposal might have. I would rather have an employee who stands side by side with me than ten feet behind me. The employee who takes ownership and takes charge is the kind of person I want on my team. As a supervisor, I know this is the kind of person who will grow with me as I grow in the company.

Notes

Stay Focused

Staying focused is not a simple task for most people. It's very easy to be distracted, especially if you're not fully committed to the task in front of you. To be successful, you have to stay focused on your goals and how you're going to achieve them. Even with your road map for success, it's easy to get distracted, especially if things aren't going as you expect.

Whenever you turn on your television, you see slim, fit celebrities who look like a million dollars. People will ask them about their secret. Most of the time, they say they watch their diet and exercise. But if you push them a little further, they usually add that their personal trainers keep them focused. Well, guess what? You don't have a personal trainer or someone to keep you focused on your path to success. If you did, you would not be reading this guide.

You would already be rich and successful. So just like that New Year's diet resolution that you might have already given up on, it's easy to give up on staying focused.

Sometimes, deep down, people want to be distracted. When I'm writing, I can't have any distractions. I need silence. Someone with my active imagination can be distracted by anything. Luckily, I have always been able to stay focused when it comes to my career.

In the workplace, I see coworkers lose their focus all the time. There are countless reasons why this happens, but for purposes of this discussion, it's not important. What is important is that, on the job, a focused person completes assignments and achieves respect from his or her superiors. Once again, for every notch you can put in that big stick you're carrying around, you're moving one step closer to achieving your goals to success.

How to stay focused:

1. For the big picture, you need to create goals for the short term and long term. It's always great if you are able to measure your success in attaining these goals.

2. When it comes to projects or events, create a checklist of what needs to be accomplished. When you have a road map in front of you, it's much easier to stay focused.

3. Distractions can be a real focus killer. The toughest distraction to deal with is coworkers. Usually the coworkers don't have a clue, or maybe they don't care if they're preventing you from completing your assignment. It may be hard, but you have to excuse

yourself from the conversation. Idle chatter is the one thing your supervisor will more than likely see, and it will definitely not help you succeed in the workplace.

It's easy to lose focus when you get knocked down and have setbacks in your career. Just remember that each day is a chance to refocus and move forward. If you stay focused, the overachievers will never see you coming.

Notes

Take Charge

When given the opportunity to take over a large assignment or manage a team of coworkers, don't squander it. Sometimes these opportunities come few and far between.

For a mild-mannered average Joe or Josie, managing a group of people will probably take you way out of your comfort zone, so managing a group of coworkers will be a challenge in itself. First of all, there could be some resentment and jealousy from those in the group who wonder why they did not get the chance to manage. Heaven forbid if there's an overachiever in the group. Although the experience may be foreign and uncomfortable, you still want to make the best of it.

You will need to take time to organize yourself and be prepared for your first meeting with the group. When you do meet with the group, don't apologize for being the new manager or team leader. On the other side of the coin, don't be arrogant or come across as too bossy. Remember, they still see you as their coworker. Present your ideas, and give direction to the group. If you open up the meeting for discussions and input, accept the positive comments as well as the negative. You should thank your coworkers and move on. You might choose to use some of the thoughts suggested in the meeting, but you might wait until you've had time to consider them in private.

Sometimes meetings can get out of control, with everyone trying to speak at the same time, small groups talking to each other, or someone trying to dominate the conversation. These are times when you will have to speak up and take back control of the meeting. This can be stressful if you have not managed anyone before, but it will get easier over time. Stay cool, calm, and collected, and manage the meeting. The thing to keep telling yourself is that this is helping you achieve your goals.

Even if this is a temporary assignment and not an actual promotion, you need to treat it as one. During this time period, don't be afraid to ask advice from your supervisor, but don't ask too often. Your supervisor might wonder if you're really up for the job. However, if you have serious doubt about an issue or a decision, do ask for advice, and then take charge and move forward. Let the supervisor see that he or she has made a wise decision by selecting you.

I do not want to oversimplify managing people. It does take time to develop your skill sets. You will have to learn to be passionate yet stern at times. You will make mistakes—but hopefully not too many. For the most part, you cannot be best friends with your employees. You are not running a popularity contest. That's not to say you won't like and respect each other.

As you commit to growth and success, there will be many more resources that can be of great help to you. This is where a general management class in a local community college or online class will be helpful.

Notes

Confrontation

Not all aspects of success have to deal with positive issues. In fact, to get ahead and stay ahead, you will have to learn how to deal with confrontation. I'm not about to say that you can turn all negative confrontations into positive results. Frankly, sometimes it's a victory that you survived the incident at all.

There can be many sources of confrontation in the business world. After all, it's life. You may have confrontations with customers, coworkers, and, yes, even supervisors. Unfortunately, it's the supervisors who may be the ones to help you move up the corporate ladder. In the business world, how you deal with confrontations can help or hurt you on your path to success. This needs to be discussed because, unlike many of the other attributes I have discussed in which you will be the catalyst for making things happen, that's not the case with confrontation. Many times, it comes to you without any warning. To be successful, you must be prepared to deal with confrontation in the most positive way you can. The confrontation may not have a positive outcome, but maybe you can diffuse it.

Confrontation is one of most difficult subjects I will discuss in this guide. Over the years, I have seen coworkers and subordinates who I believe should advance up the corporate ladder hold themselves back over this issue. It is very real, with next to no attention paid to it. Most issues related to conflict are dealt with only after an explosion has occurred.

The bottom line is, when a confrontation takes place, the spotlight is on the participants. Top management is usually keenly aware when some type of confrontation has taken place. Believe me—if they see you have handled the issue, they will take notice. If you're successful, then they won't have to deal with the problem. Later in the guide, I will discuss keeping a cool head.

There are three classic types of confrontations; you have probably been through all of them already. The first one is customer confrontations, better known as customer service. The old adage "The customer is always right" usually is correct. When customers are right, for the most part there should not even be a confrontation. However, the problem occurs when they want extra compensation, the solution is not perfectly clear, they are unreasonable in their demands, or they are truly not right. In most cases, an apology will help lower the tone of the confrontation. Let the customer speak his or her mind—but, hopefully, off to the side. You don't want to become a sideshow for others to watch. Your goal in this scenario is to satisfy the customer at least in part. There will be some customers who, for whatever reason, will not accept anything you say. At this point, try to be as polite as you can, and end the confrontation. In this case, there will be no winner. One thing you have to remember is that you have to deal with the customer and the issue. You cannot get upset and simply walk away from the confrontation. Or you might just have to pass the customer up to a higher supervisor.

The coworker confrontation is a losing scenario for both employees. Often, both employees lose control of their emotions—and nothing good will come from this. It's best to walk away from coworker confrontations as quickly as possible. These confrontations can be devastating to your career. If need be, report the incident to your supervisor, and move on.

The third type of confrontation should just never happen. A confrontation with your supervisor is pretty much a deathblow to your path of success with the company. You might just have to sit there and take a verbal beating and afterward shake it off. The first question to ask yourself afterward is, "Did I deserve this?" If not, there are other avenues to address your grievance.

I have a good example of a customer-service confrontation. A customer purchased several lumber products from a retailer for a DIY home-repair job—so much that a truck was needed to deliver it to his home. After the trucker left, the customer discovered that some of the material was not what he had ordered. He went back to the retailer, demanding a refund of his one-hundred-dollar delivery fee. He also demanded the correct material that he had paid for.

If you noticed I've been using the word "demanding," that's because he was yelling at the salespeople who sold him the products. At this point the supervisor was called, and he correctly asked the customer to move off to the side so they could talk. The supervisor asked the customer to stop yelling so they could resolve the issue. The customer was still so mad that he stomped away briefly, before returning.

An observant employee who had been watching the confrontation stepped into the discussion and asked what the customer was using the material for. Still angry, the customer explained his project. The employee smiled and told the customer that although the material was not what he ordered, it was the correct material for the job. Actually, what he had ordered was not the proper material. The other good news was that the cost of the product was almost identical. The customer was satisfied and actually apologized for yelling.

The lesson here is that yes, the supervisor might have eventually defused the confrontation. However, an observant employee stepped in and calmly and quickly resolved the situation. You can be sure that the supervisor took note of what the employee did: I was the supervisor, and I did take note.

The old saying "It takes two to tango" is true. Spend time on your career and your path to success, and avoid those who do not share that same philosophy. Your career will blossom much more quickly.

Notes

The World of Sales

Sales is such a large profession that spreads across all industries, so I could not resist spending time on the sales profession. Why? Because it is dominated by extroverted overachievers. Every day when you step away from your home or workplace, you are in contact with sales professionals at all levels. Sales is an honorable profession, and I have spent many years in the industry. There are all different types of sales positions available, from the salesperson in a department store to the car-dealership salesperson or the corporate salesperson who makes million-dollar deals.

Many retail-store-level salespeople are new entries into the workforce. This type of position usually provides a salary with some small sales incentives. They are very good and safe jobs. The next level of sales tends to offer a low base salary with much higher incentives with high turnovers. An example would be new-car salespersons. The last level is for the big hitters. The base and the incentives are both very high. This is the playground for overachievers. The bottom line is this: overachievers are probably worth hiring, but then again, so are you.

The sales profession is worth spending time on because, for the most part, you don't need a specialized college degree to become a salesperson. Most companies will provide the necessary training for you to become proficient in selling their products or services.

The overachievers are very well equipped for this profession, especially the big-hitter type of sales. They can be very aggressive, outgoing, and likable and are not afraid to close the sale and ask for the order. Yes, that all sounds great, and it is, but maybe you feel you don't fit those criteria. That might be true, but neither did I when I was in this type of sales. In a large sales company, I never broke into the top 10 percent of the sales force, but I did crack the top 25 percent of the sales force. I discovered that in short-duration sales promotions, I could actually be the number-one sales producer 40 to 50 percent of the time.

So how in the heck can an average Joe or Josie compete with and even outproduce the big hitters? Sounds impossible, right? Not really. You just have to develop your own game plan and strategies that work within the guidelines I have already discussed. I'll outline a few sales pointers below, but feel free to adapt them to your style.

Successful sales points to remember:

1. Be early for all your appointments. Many sales representatives tend to be late. Plan your schedule

days ahead of time, and prepare for the appointment.

2. Be prepared to do business, and know your product inside and out. The worst thing you can do is guess or call someone for the answer.

3. Be a good listener. Most sales reps spend too much time talking and not enough time listening.

4. Don't pressure for an order. Odds are, you might not be good at that anyway. When I was in sales, I developed a strong sales pitch so that I never had to pressure for the order. I relied on my ability to convince the customers during the sales pitch to want to close the order themselves. I was never comfortable with pressuring for an order, so I didn't.

5. If you say you're going to do something like mail the customer samples, then do it. Follow-up is key. Many sales reps are terrible with the follow-up details.

6. The bigger the sale, the less likely you'll actually close it on the first sales call. You will have to cultivate the potential sale and gain the respect of the customer.

7. Always send a follow-up e-mail to thank customers for their time or the order.

8. When you do get the order, make sure your company processes it properly, and keep the customer updated with the progress of the order.

9. Find topics of interest with all of your customers. You're not looking to be their best friend, but a friendly relationship is good. It's nice if they're glad to see you instead of thinking, "Oh, what's this guy going to try to sell me this time?"

10. Research your competitors. Know their strengths, weaknesses, programs, and products. Play your strengths off their weaknesses. Don't try to close a sale by demeaning your competitors.

Notes

_____

_____

_____

_____

_____

_____

_____

_____

_____

_____

_____

_____

Technology Skills

Today's world is very technology oriented. Workstations, laptops, tablets, smartphones, and, yes, even smart watches affect everything we do in the world today. For those of you under fifty years of age, you've probably already used the devices I mentioned above. For those of you over fifty, you might not have embraced the technological revolution in the same way as the younger generations.

No matter what your level of experience and comfort with technology are, you must embrace technology if you plan on moving up the corporate ladder. Kids are growing up in the world with no fear of electronics of any type; in fact, they embrace everything electronic. If you shy away from computers and other devices, now is the time to get over it. Your future will depend on it, even if you're just riding out your career. I understand you might think that this subject doesn't belong in this discussion, but believe me, it does. The overachievers and the generations coming up after you have or will have mastered their skill sets in this area.

I can pretty much guarantee you this: the overachievers of the world are also probably very savvy when it comes to electronics and IT. You will have to up your game in this field just to be competitive, much less excel. At this point, I can tell what you're thinking: "I'm screwed." Well, only if you don't do anything about it. In almost any business field, you are going to need at least an average knowledge of computers and software. That shouldn't be hard; after all, we're average Joes and Josies.

Kidding aside, most of you probably do have some type of a computer or smart device, and you probably surf the Internet in some fashion.

If you don't already have Microsoft Office on your home computer, you should buy a copy. Most computer-related tasks at work will involve one of the Office programs or something similar. For most of you, this might be boring, but you need to be proficient with this type of software to succeed in the business world.

The programs include the following:

1. Outlook: This is the e-mail software that most businesses use. There are many other packages for e-mail, but you will have to understand the e-mail process.

2. Word: This is the most common type of word-processing program on the market. Again, you will need to understand this software.

3. Excel: This software will be found for the most part in the fields of accounting, sales and purchasing, and inventory. Working with spreadsheets takes a little more expertise, but it is worthwhile to become familiar with Excel. This will give you an edge, because many people do not use it.

4. PowerPoint and Access are both also part of the Office suite. In most cases, you would not be expected to know these applications.

If they're involved in sales or purchasing, many businesses will use some type of customized database software. It is very important be able to navigate this type of software. Most types of database software are fairly simple and straightforward to use. If you're uncomfortable with any of the above applications, someone you know might be of help, and local community colleges usually offer entry-level courses. Some local libraries or other government agencies also offer classes. There are even online tutorials you can do by yourself.

The more proficient you are with computers and related devices, in conjunction with your other attributes, the better your odds are of climbing up the corporate ladder. As long as you're thinking positive and looking forward, you will not have any issues mastering your technology skills.

The world of technology is constantly changing. You always need to set aside a little time to catch up on what's new. Just when you think some newfangled device has nothing to do with you, your company may embrace it twelve months later. As I look back over the years, I realize all the technologies I was weaned on—the big, dominant software applications of the day—are no longer in business or were absorbed by other companies. Every day is a new day when it comes to technology. Keep your mind open, and embrace technology. It will become one of the skill sets that will help you succeed now and into the future.

Notes

Self-Improvement

These are self-improvement points that will help get you noticed and maybe help advance your career. Whether you're a blue-collar or white-collar employee doesn't really matter; many of these self-improvement points will be of help.

Self-improvement points:

1. Lose the "It's not my job" syndrome, and become part of the team. Not doing so sends a clear signal to management that you have not bought into the company and are just there putting in your time.

2. Go the extra mile; additional effort will surprise and impress your superiors. This is when you not only

finish the project but also see something else that can be done to enhance the results.

3. Be positive, appreciate your job, and grow with the company. If you can't feel comfortable doing this, then you're probably with the wrong company. This refers back to the comments I made earlier about the glass being half empty or half full. Supervisors can spot a bad attitude from a mile away. Believe me, they always want the positive person on their team.

4. Smile at work. It is contagious, and your superiors will notice. Trust me: a smile is worth a thousand words, especially if you lean toward the introverted side. A smile sets the stage for positive things to happen.

5. Volunteer to do more when the company hits rough patches. It's the old saying, "When the going gets tough, the tough get going." It is very noticeable when someone leaves early or chooses not to stay late to finish up a project.

6. Suggest improvements that can help the company with increased efficiency and productivity. A good supervisor will always want to hear suggestions from an employee. Many times, the best ideas come from the least expected places. Let that surprise be you.

7. Remove your blinders, and try to see the whole picture—not just your place in the company. This will give you a big edge over other employees. This topic is so important that I could never say enough about it. If you do get a promotion and have

blinders on, you will not succeed at your new position. You have to see the big picture to succeed in growing with any company.

8. Don't let negative or apathetic coworkers pull you down to their level. Keep that glass half full, and plow forward. As they say, "Misery loves company." Let the miserable ones be by themselves.

9. Keep abreast of changes and new technologies in your industry. You need every edge you can muster. As I have already said—and it's worth repeating— you will have to embrace technology to succeed. Your future depends on it.

10. Complete all assignments to the best of your abilities. Never take shortcuts that may backfire and

reflect poorly on you. If an assignment is worth doing, it's worth doing right.

For the most part, these self-improvement points are all things you can instantly embrace. Let these points become part of your life. You will never regret the decision.

Notes

The Go-To Person

Always try to be the go-to person in your organization. Be known to your superiors as the one they can count on to see an assignment through—not just the big projects, but especially the small ones too. A portfolio of accomplished small projects can be just as or more important than a large project. I know it might sound like I'm asking you to be the gal or guy Friday, but I'm not. In the world of business, a good supervisor will delegate assignments. One of the worst things for a career is when an employee is given an assignment and doesn't follow through on it.

If a supervisor knows you're the go-to person who has his or her back, that increases your credibility. Don't worry—you will not be taken for granted, but appreciated.

Benefits to your future if you are a go-to person:

1. You're learning discipline to complete assignments. In the world of business, one of the cogs that drive a company is the sheer number of assignments happening simultaneously. If you complete assignments in a timely fashion, your star will shine.

2. You're getting insights into management's thinking. As you gain the trust of management, you will start to get a glimmer into their thinking process. Pay attention to this; it will be a fantastic learning tool that will speed your advancement.

3. You're learning that the devil is sometimes in the details. Many small pieces to the puzzle are as important as the big ones. As I've stated, in the business world you need to see and understand the big picture,

but at the same time it's the small details that drive the big events. It's the small actions that make the big ones work. Pay attention.

4. You'll begin to appreciate and better understand what it takes to develop and execute projects at the management level. When you get to this point, you're ready for that next level of success.

5. Your supervisor will develop a confidence in you that will lead to a better future. A good supervisor may hate to see you advance because you are so valuable to him or her, but when it comes down to it, a supervisor like that will want only the best for a valued employee.

Notes:

Just Do It

Many supervisors and overachievers have the "Just Do It" philosophy and attitude when dealing with a project that needs to be completed. All supervisors have a moment when they feel someone else can't tackle the project properly, so they simply give up and do it themselves. Some supervisors are just going to do it no matter what anyway. I'll pick back up on this shortly.

As an average Joe or Josie, at times you will need to take the same stance. It's like walking by a piece of paper on the floor while fellow employees stand around. Why does no one stop and pick it up? They might be lazy. Maybe it's the "it's not my job" syndrome. It could be that they don't care, or maybe they're blind in one eye and can't see out of the other. The point is, most everyone sees the piece of paper, and sooner or later someone is going to take the initiative to pick it up. Unfortunately, it will probably be a supervisor or the cleaning staff.

I know—what's this got to do with success? Everything! As I've said before, you need to remove those blinders and pay attention to your career and the workplace around you. If you start training yourself to see things that are out of place or not right and then do something about it, your supervisors and management team will take notice. Many of these things are small and go unnoticed, but remember that true change and progress are usually achieved one step at a time. Make sure you're the one to pick up that piece of paper, and be on the lookout for the obvious that everyone else is missing.

As you strive for success, this is a great attribute to develop, but take warning: the higher up the corporate ladder you climb, the more you will depend on others. You will need to start delegating jobs and authority. So, someday you will be looking at other up-and-coming average Joes and Josies who will have the same "Just Do It" attitude. This will help all of you on your path to future successes.

Notes:

Common Sense

As you begin to reflect on your career or your first career opportunity, think about some of these points. They have nothing to do with being an overachiever but are good old common-sense points to practice that will help you improve your chances of getting a new job or improving your status with your employer.

1. Be a problem solver and not a problem causer. Never point out a problem unless you can offer a solution for it. People who point out problems with no thought of a solution are doomed to end up as one of the problems. Negative people point out problems without offering solutions. Positive people point out problems *and* their solutions.

2. Having an ego is a great thing, but remember, a strong ego can allow you to create personal goals that are not realistic. I have a large but kind of silent ego, which causes me to do exactly what I'm warning against. To be honest, I have missed many goals I set, but that's fine. I can accept that, and usually I get fairly close, so I don't take coming up short as a negative. I let it go and look forward to the next challenge. Try to set your goals realistically; your ego does like to win sometimes.

3. Always be early for all business events and appointments. Being on time doesn't set you apart from the pack, but being early for appointments does. If you're going to be late for appointments, please ask for a refund for this guide. It's that important to be early. Since I spent a large portion of my life on an island, some people I've known

will use the excuse for being late, "Well, you know, it's island time." To me, living on a beautiful island is a blessing—not an excuse. Be early, and show people you care about who you are and what you represent.

4. Be a good listener, and speak when the moment is right. There's nothing worse in a business meeting than when people are babbling on and trying to dominate the conversation. Making it worse, they go off message and start talking about something unrelated. When you're having a meeting with others, respect their time. Their time is valuable too.

5. Remember what got you to this point in your life. Keep the good attributes, throw out the bad ones, and develop additional new good ones. Another saying I will never forget from John Cotter was,

"Remember who brung you to the dance." He actually meant the saying in a different way than what it means to me. To me, it means you always remember the good attributes that got you this far in life. They will be just as useful going forward in future adventures.

6. Keep control of your negative emotions. Relate to this: when you're in a traffic jam, what do people start doing first? Yes, they honk their horns. As soon as that starts, everything spirals out of control, and you have deadlock. Nothing is gained by losing your temper. Stay cool and calm, and don't honk your horn. The calmer mind will prevail nine out of ten times. Let that always be you.

7. Speaking in front of a group of any size can be very intimidating for anyone, especially for someone

with an introverted personality. In high school and college, I enrolled in speech classes. I truly feared the idea of standing in front of the class and reciting my speeches, but something told me back then that someday this painful experience might be worth the effort, and it was.

I'll pass on a few tips that have helped me over the years. The most important point is to be familiar with the subject matter. The more you know for the speech, whether you learn it on the job, through a personal interest, or through extensive research, the less stressful it will be giving the speech. Practice and time yourself. Know the time allocation you are expected to fill. Giving the speech over and over in front of a mirror will help immensely.

In my past experiences, if the speech was on a

subject matter I did not know extremely well, I would write it out and memorize it word for word. However, if it was a subject matter I was familiar with, then I would create a simple outline of bullet points to speak from. I always found this type of speech much easier to give, as the outline allowed me to comfortably interject outside thoughts during the speech. The good news is, the more you speak in front of a group of people, the easier it gets. You'll always be slightly nervous until you get out that first sentence, but after that, you'll be great.

8. Set goals and objectives daily, weekly, and monthly. They can be personal or job related. As I have stated before, try to make them realistic and attainable. You're not always going to achieve them, but don't get down on yourself if you don't. Remember that tomorrow is another day.

9. Open your blinders. All too often—and I see it every day—we only see what's in front of us. Our perspective is only what affects us. Most supervisors would give their left arm if any of their subordinates could see the broader picture of the company as their job is related to it. Take a little extra time to study and ask questions to better understand how you fit in the grand scheme of the company. Your superiors will see you in a totally new light and will be able to envision you with promotions and expanded roles in the company.

10. Dress for success, especially in the interview process. The old saying that you only have one chance to make a good first impression is absolutely true. In the interview process, the overachievers are going to stand out no matter what—most of the time

in a good way, but sometimes not so good. They might be too aggressive, which might not be perceived as a good attribute. They might also be terrible listeners and talk too much in an interview. So be observant, be polite, and don't be afraid to speak up and demonstrate to the interviewer that you took time to research the company and the position you're applying for. Finally, make sure that you have a very professional résumé.

Notes

_____

_____

_____

_____

_____

_____

_____

_____

_____

_____

_____

What Works for You

Remember, this is a guide to success—not a road map to success. You will have to eventually build your own road map to follow; after all, you're the only one who truly knows where you want to go. As you have read through this guide, I believe you've likely found many recommendations you will be able to try in your current position. You might be comfortable with some of these recommendations, and you might not be so sure about others. Start out slow, and define your strategies and goals. Some of your goals will not be apparent this early on, but they will develop over time.

Since many of my suggestions are very simple to begin practicing, go ahead and start using them. There's no rush. Rome wasn't built in a day, and your self-improvements won't be either. Right now, remember what I said in the

145

subtitle: "The brilliant overachievers will never see you coming." They're not even aware you're out there. The timetable is on your side, so use your new skill sets wisely and in a timely way. This will be a process over the long haul, but the rewards and success will start showing little by little.

For those of you who are going through the interview process, the timetable is different. I hope these thoughts will work for you. Because you only have one chance to make a good first impression in the interview process, you will need to be more organized early on. Get some help on your résumé, because you want one that will get you that first interview. Don't make your résumé too long, but be informative. Take time to research the company you're interviewing with. Google is a great tool to use for research. Dress for success; wear your Sunday best. Be early for the interview. It's better that you are kept waiting than the HR personnel. Speak up, answer the questions clearly, and, based on your research, ask a few questions about the position and the company. Impress upon the interviewer that you'll be a great addition to the company and that you're anxious to work and be a team player.

Notes

Faith

These final few paragraphs are for those faith-driven average Joes and Josies who believe in a higher being. The nonbelievers may also enjoy the read. Who knows—you might have second thoughts. No, this is not where I try to make a convert out of you, but faith can be very important in your life, including in success with a career.

Many business owners, although they might not show it, believe that faith and compassion are essential parts of their business.

For many years, I felt uncomfortable asking God for assistance and guidance with work-related issues like finding a job or improving my career. I believed he could guide me in my personal life, but I felt it was greedy to ask for help when it came to my career. As usual, through the school of hard knocks, I found out otherwise—that he is there for us in all aspects of our life. The good Lord will always be there for us and is an excellent listener. I do seek his guidance daily—yes, even about business-related decisions.

The bottom line is this: Do you want to go it alone, or would you like guidance and support from God, who has guided millions of average Joes and Josies throughout the millennia? The answer is for you to choose.

Having read this guide, it's now time for you to create your own road map for success. Your destiny is in your hands, you have the tools and the knowledge to move forward. Life is an adventure and your determination, drive, and a positive attitude will help you accomplish your goals. Your future is waiting for you, the brilliant overachievers will never see you coming.

No matter what your endeavor, I wish you success, and
may God bless you.

R. C. Dressed for Success

Novels by R. C. Farrington

The Crystal Pendulum—Guardian of the Bermuda Triangle

Shadows of Black Bayou

Blood Fangs—The Beast Huntress

The Life and Times of the Bayou Banditos

Blood Fangs—Quest for the Dark One

Phantom Marauders of the Bermuda Triangle

Death Diamonds of Bermudez

The Isle of Devils Holy War

Spinners I—The Lost Treasure of Bermuda

Spinners II—The Protectors of the Bermuda Triangle

Spinners III—Curse of the Bermuda Abyss